I AM WILLING

The Invitation of Christ

DEAN KNIGHT

With

Michael J Spyker

About Miracles and More

AgapeDeum

Published in Adelaide, Australia by AgapeDeum
Contact: agapedeum.com

ISBN   978-0-6488957-4-9

Publication assistance by Immortalise

Cover design: Ben Morton

CONTENT

Hello!

We are living in turbulent times with the Lord impressing on my spirit that it won't get any easier. As Christians we need to strengthen our inner person in Christ through prayer. The Lord is willing and close by, always. Only with help from the Holy Spirit will we be truly able to cope with the future. Of this I am convinced and hopefully my little book will encourage you to have confidence in God's providence and care. Get close to Jesus and with him face all that comes your way. God loves you and is faithful.

Dean Knight

1

The Book

It was a sunny morning with summer almost gone. Dean looked out over the calm sea.

'I began to feel distinctly strange, out of breath and dizzy,' he said. 'No energy to walk further than the corner of our street. Best to check in at the hospital. An artery to my heart was 95% blocked up. With a reduced medical staff on the weekend they rushed to operate nevertheless. You know what they told me afterwards? I had actually died while they put in the stent. There was a 100% blockage then. Wonderful, I said. You brought me back to life. I once revived someone who was well beyond resuscitation. Through Prayer.' Dean gave that chuckle, as only he can.

That's Dean for you. Did I believe him? Such a miracle? Had to. Dean is fearless in the pursuit of what God can do, without guile and never tells a lie. For many years we had lost contact. I met him at church decades ago, where I was a Pastor. But life moved on. Dean continued on his journey guided by the Lord affecting many people. I ended up in academia with a special interest in spiritual theology. Now we sat together sipping coffees, old friends, at the seafront in Adelaide, South Australia, our home town.

'I must write a book,' Dean said. A comment he had made at our first meeting some time ago. We had not met since. Writing a book is never easy, while publishing is an involved business. I am familiar with both and had decided to help out. Over many years Dean filled up journals recording his happenings with the Lord. Insights gained and strange events that occurred. Journals are good source material. A book though needs a selective and structured focus.

'*I Am Willing*. That's the title.' Dean underlined those words in an open journal before him. 'For God is most willing!'

His enthusiasm never fails. Neither does his conviction. It struck me as a fine title for a book as it cuts in two ways. God is ever present and willing. But am I willing also, to take Christian life seriously? A double dynamic that was central in how Jesus walked on earth. God willingly offered miracles to raise awareness of a divine presence in the Son. Jesus then told stories and gave advice about how to live in ways pleasing to God. Those who followed Jesus simply because of his miraculous power, and they were many, he quickly discouraged.

I Am Willing takes a similar approach. The great things God is doing still today will be told and celebrated. Dean has much to share. But Jesus is the one to follow, and a growing in the fruit of the spirit is expected. God is willing and an ever helping hand in trouble. The miraculous, when it occurs, is a clear sign of that, while a solid grip on life with a willingness to tap into God's power within, is likewise a miracle. A quiet and continuing one. Both sides of God's presence will be presented in *I Am Willing*.

It is Dean's book in which to tell his incredible stories and express his concerns. The stories will include some reflections on vibrant Christian living derived from my years of learning and discovery. There are ways whereby to ensure a spirit awareness in every day. It develops into a special friendship with the Lord – a grace enablement.

'I wish I could leave my name out of this whole thing,' Dean said. 'All the glory belongs to God.' On that point we understood each other perfectly.

He got up from his chair. 'Sorry, Michael. Got to go. A girl asked me to come and pray with her.'

That's my friend, Dean.

2

Spiritual Intelligence

Dean was sitting at the dining room table at home. His lanky frame slightly bent forward and a stack of journals at hand. 'Here,' he said, 'this is what I have written these last few months,' and handed me a hard cover notebook. Over a hundred pages of memories jotted down in pencil. 'Kathy told me off, you know, about exaggerating what I said about my stay in hospital.' Dean and Kathy have been married for five decades and she had read my account of our recent meeting. 'She insists that the doctor never said I had actually died, but just that my heart had stopped.' Dean shrugged his shoulders. 'Perhaps that's right,' he admitted. 'But then, when your heart stops you're dead, I suppose.' I agreed that indeed it depended how you looked at it.

People come to their reality differently – how they digest information and talk about it. Many years ago, I attended a revival-like meeting with Winkie Pratney as speaker. He expressed how he used to become frustrated when dealing with artistic people, he himself being the logical, factual type. In bringing his irritation before God he was told: 'Winkie, I'm an artist!' It changed his attitude and he was a better man for it.

I can relate to that firsthand. My wife at times tells me about things starting right in the middle of the story. Somehow I will have to figure out the beginning. As a linear story teller myself her habit used to annoy me. But no longer. I began to understand that her mind is focussed on that part of the story she is feeling herself through and it becomes verbalised first. Apart from confusing the hearer there is nothing wrong with that. My wife is an artistic type – a writer of children's stories, a drawer, dressmaker and more.

Dean, who is very much a feeling person, gives me that impression of experiencing life a little differently from the normal, as if in his thinking there is a partial disconnect from what confronts him. It is deceptive for he is quite engaged at the same time. In this he was misunderstood already as a child. School work was not Dean's strength. He found it difficult to memorise data. Perhaps he gave an impression of being a dreamer. At age 13 his IQ was measured. It was a popular method in determining a person's ability in those days that concentrated on logical intelligence. The value of emotional intelligence and other types was as yet unheard of. Young Dean was present while the results were discussed with his father. The verdict was none too flattering. He would be destined for the factory floor or in a sales department. As well-meant as it might have been to find out what Dean would be about, to have it spoken out over you as an early teenager was bound to leave its scars. Being naturally tough and tenacious, Dean decided to set his goals and prove them all wrong. 'I ended up having my own business,' he told me. 'By age 30, I had everything they said I would never get. A well-to-do life.' But still today, in certain conversations, Dean is prone to say: 'I'm not very clever.' Childhood wounds burrow deeply.

When Dean sets out to achieve something he tends to get there. Necessary sacrifices do not daunt him. During his teenage years he took up speed walking and became the youngest participant ever to be selected for the trial that would determine the 1964 Australian Olympic team. It made for good newspaper copy, more so because Dean was expected to win the trail. 'But when I was at the starting line of the trial my world came crashing down,' he explained. 'Suddenly I was told I had been disqualified. The organisers, who included my father, explained that being 17 years old was too young to compete at the 50 km distance. For that an Olympic speed walker needed to be 19 at the minimum, which they had overlooked. I fell into a deep hole.'

He found his solace in riding a BSA 650 motorbike and for 8 months became a 'rocker'. Dean hit the town in leathers. Then, much to his father's delight, he sold the bike. He missed the training and began speed walking once more, this time seeking to qualify for the Commonwealth Games in the UK. All was on track when another blow struck, even harder than the first one. Australia had joined in sending troops to the Vietnam War. Those soldiers were conscripted by ballot. 'My name came up,' Dean said. 'Again, all my effort had been for nothing.' He will not talk about the killing fields of Vietnam. Like all war veterans Dean tries to forget. But it never fully worked and years later, back in Australia, repatriation doctors often had him visit psychiatrists. How helpful that was remains an open question.

I knew, Dean had returned seriously wounded. From his notebook I learned it happened in a battle at "Corral", on the 8th of May, 1968. Medical transport flew him back to Australia for a long recuperation. That he felt let down by his own country, Dean is happy to discuss. It is the story of most Vietnam vets, who society preferred to forget about. The media remained silent about the horrors of that war and people in the street had little idea of it. 'While lying suffering on my sickbed I received a phone call from my employer before the war,' Dean said. 'It was disgusting. Not even one word of encouragement or sympathy for how I had fought for my country with my mates in life destroying circumstances and not of our own free will. No "thank you" for that. Just urging me to get back to work soon. By law they had to hold my position open while I was in Vietnam, but not now anymore. It was totally heartless.'

These days Dean walks a little lopsidedly and in pain. I asked whether that was still an aftereffect of the war. Not so. It was arthritis in his hip lately, probably because of his speed walking when young. For years after returning from Vietnam though his war wounds had kept on given him many problems. 'Until the Lord healed me which became the catalyst for my salvation,' Dean said. 'I could walk freely again and from then on decided to do so for the Lord.'

Dean is a walking miracle. The same tenacity he brought to his Olympic dreams, he has applied to his work for God over the years. Dean may appear a little removed from life's immediacy, but that is not so. He is simply always focused on the Lord's presence first. In many ways Dean is an artist of the spirit. Artists look at life differently. They see and sense things that others don't. It doesn't make matters any less real and some-times more so. Dean has a higher spiritual intelligence than most people. He perceives and understands the Holy Spirit in special ways and is willing to act on what is shown with the courage of faith. Many have been blessed by it.

3

The Weather God

Dean has seen God work miraculously many times over many years. He never tires of telling of it. I knew that some involved weather events and I asked him about that.

'Three come to mind,' he said. 'The first one was at the Murray River about an hour from Adelaide. I was helping a member of our church add a room to his shack near the water. We were busy pouring a concrete foundation when it began to rain. "Well, that's it," my friend said. The sky looked black and threatening. I had a check in my spirit. Something told me that this is the Lord's Day and the Lord would be happy to see the floor finished. I took my lead from the Holy Spirit and cried out, "Hear me clouds in this sky. You may let your water fall, but not where I am standing. Rain onto the shacks on the left and the right and over the river but not here." All of a sudden the rain stopped.'

'That's quite a story,' I commented, stating the obvious.

'Well, yes.' Dean is always reluctant to accept any kind of praise or admiration. 'We had plenty of concrete sand but ran out of cement. Arriving in the nearby town for supply they asked us what we were doing for it was bucketing water from the sky. They thought we were nuts doing concrete work that day. It kept on raining until we arrived at the shack where the sky was clear. We finished the job.'

'Just in time for more rain,' I suggested.

'That's what my friend thought. He began to cover the floor with corrugated iron sheets. I told him that the floor didn't need earthly protection. Staying over at the shack for the night it rained often. In the morning we found the floor perfectly hardened and not pitted. Not a drop of rain would have landed on it.'

'That's amazing.' What else could I say?

'God is able,' Dean simply said.

I know that Dean spends many hours with the Lord. Obviously, the Lord has singled him out for this kind of ministry. Not that this makes it easy for him. Often Dean has to put his neck on the line, as we would call it. Once, Australia was suffering one of its severe droughts with water restrictions in many places. Dean became fed-up with it and asked the Lord what he would have to do to solve this problem. 'The Lord said, "What problem? If you're anxious for nothing, there is no problem. So, bring it to nothing."

'So what did you do?' I asked.

'I asked the people of our little church to come and stand outside with me and face east. I explained to them what the Lord had told me and we decided to fix the problem of drought. We prayed and declared it to have ended.

'Next day, I drove with a friend to Melbourne. A stay of a few days. We carried those prayers with us in expectation. About an hour in on the way back to Adelaide, near Ballarat, we felt to say, "Now Lord, now!" The skies had clouded over. All of a sudden it began to rain. I learned later that it had bucketed in Ballarat with a river running through the main street. The drought had been broken in a large part of Australia.'

Then Dean continued with another story about the weather. This one about an even more severe situation. For years my wife and I had a place north of Adelaide in a country town situated in the Flinders Ranges. Close to it were many inaccessible mountain valleys that had collected dead wood for over a 100 years. One summer, with the hot land brittle, a fire broke out because of dry lightning. To this day we shudder at the power of blazing hills. Trees exploded like fire balls far up into the air. The fire burned for weeks. We observed this over a distance, of course. Fortunately our town was spared due to the heroic effort of the fire brigade helped by the local farmers and a wind change. Bush fires are a constant threat around Australia. Dean knows all about that.

Some years ago, Kathy and Dean were staying with friends on Philip Island near Melbourne. A call came in to say that close to their friend's property in the vicinity of Ararat a very dangerous fire was burning right through the paddocks. Dean explained what happened.

'They ran a sheep and grain farm there which

was in line of the blaze. Their farm manager told them that the animals were in danger of being burned to death and there was little that could be done about it. Neighbouring farms had already lost countless of sheep. Needless to say, our friends were distraught and felt helpless.'

Forrest fires and grass ones, they can all be deadly.

'The Lord reminded me, I was given a scripture that very morning in prayer that would help change the situation. I prayed with my friends that the wind might blow the fire away from their property. That is what happened. The fire passed by a few metres from their lengthy fence and all the animals were safe. Not so those on farms nearby.'

Dean took a break. He went to the kitchen for a glass of water, and continued.

'I sensed in my spirit that the word God had given me was not as yet exhausted. So I commanded the skies to weep over the land and simply put the fire out. Then it began to rain over the Ararat area.'

The local paper, Ararat Advertiser, on January 9,

2015, reported as follows. "About 2 pm we had about five millimetres of rain and that dampened things down. Embers were falling on damp grass and going out."

'Most surprisingly, it rained out of a blue sky,' Dean said.

Dean had well and truly got my attention. I was aware that major fires could create their own weather systems. Whether Dean's kind of miracle fits that category, I didn't know.

'Something else happened,' Dean said. 'I learned about it later, from a good friend. He and his wife, who suffers from asthma, were bound to travel through Ararat on their way home to Adelaide. They were advised to delay their journey because of the thick smoke over that town. Bush fires were burning so fiercely that its smoke was noticeable in Melbourne. Half an hour later they were contacted again with the information that miraculously the heavens had cleared and it had rained out of a blue sky. While driving through Ararat my friend, who much loves the Lord, casually asked in prayer how this could happen. The Lord said, "One of my servants placed a demand on my word urging me to perform it." My friend asked who would do such a thing. The Lord said, "You know him as Dean Knight."'

With Dean, the Lord impresses a scripture upon him to apply in given situations. That becomes the basis for his declarations towards healing and change. 'You know what scripture I got the morning of the fire,' he asked. 'Proverbs 12:10. "A righteous man regards the life of his animals"'

It became the stepping stone towards amazing events.

'Once a scripture locks itself into my being in a special way, then the outcomes become inescapable if I press the Lord to act on what I have received,' Dean explained.

In this divine way he has helped many people over decades.

4

On the Edge

A large container ship was at anchor on the horizon waiting for a call-in from Port Adelaide. A stiff south westerly crested the waves with white. Looking out towards the sea, Dean and I were sitting sheltered from the wind on my balcony at home. The sky was clouded over the Adelaide coast but mostly blue above the waters. A nice enough day. 'I don't get it,' Dean said. 'Not then, not before, and not now,' his voice toned with some disappointment and despondency.

He had just told me about having been invited for the first time to join a group playing golf and on that day to have healed a man with terminal throat cancer. Neil riding along in a buggy mentioned it to be his last game because of this illness. 'Not on my watch,' Dean had responded jumping into the cart. 'Jesus will heal you.' Dean prayed with Neil in the knowledge that earlier that morning the Lord had impressed the story of Jesus turning water into wine upon him. To everyone's amazement Neil was back playing golf one week later. He was fully healed with every sign of the cancer having disappeared. After a month he confided in Dean about the feeling that he should really tell people about what had happened. Dean invited Neil to accept Christ, but he declined. Now years later Neil is still playing golf cancer free and his fellow golfers, Dean included, still talk about it. None of them though have become Christians.

It is so totally unlike Dean's own response when the Lord healed his shot-up back from Vietnam.

'What was your experience like when becoming healed,' I asked.

'Yeah, my problem was far greater than a sore throat, though that was bad on Neil,' Dean said. 'My back was so painful that I couldn't sit at a desk for long. For a full six years I was back in hospital regularly for treatment. The horrors of Vietnam kept playing up in my memories. Nothing undermines your identity quite like fighting in a war, I would think.'

During those six painful years Dean married Kathy and they lost their first child because of a miscarriage. While soon after Dean's father, whom he loved dearly, got run over by a drunken driver whilst stepping out of a chicken shop. His father ended up in hospital and died of meningitis. The early years of their marriage were difficult. Bad events were happening all around and Dean struggled greatly with his health. Kathy and he were desperately learning to live together. Kathy is some lady, hanging in there with a deeply troubled man.

'At one point I became suicidal, you know,' Dean told me.

We talked about it.

Dean had been able to build a successful life around selling insurance. A nicely furnished home and an expensive car were some of the benefits. After Kathy's miscarriage they had two more children, a girl and a boy. But both had health difficulties in their early years, which Dean put down to him having been exposed to Agent Orange in Vietnam. As the years progressed Dean's health worsened. He remembered lying on the floor unable to move until a chiropractor visited him at home and manipulated his back to ease the pain. At the repatriation hospital they tried all kinds of operative procedures to alleviate his suffering. Dean told me how he could see his marriage falling apart. He was no longer able to make much of a living. Slowly anything valuable he owned was sold off to put bread on the table.

'One night, my mind snapped,' he said. 'Earlier that day I had gone to a pawn shop with the crazy idea of selling my Vietnam medals, but something stopped me. I got back home wondering how to buy some food, when I saw Kathy busy at the ironing board. She was freshening up the clothes of our children. At the thought of an iron and a board being worth money for groceries at a pawn shop my mind gave way.'

Dean still finds it difficult to deal with that memory. He escaped from the house, got into their borrowed car, and drove up the steeply winding road towards Morialta Falls in the Adelaide foothills. The moment to end it all was near.

There is a fair bit of birdlife around our home, easily noticed as our living room and deck are one storey up. I noticed a small bird flying by. It reminded me of a black bird that used to sing beautifully in one of the trees close by. It is amazing the sound such a small bird can make and so effortlessly. It lifts the spirit. Why that thought occurred to me with Dean telling such a serious story I don't know.

'The way I remember it, is that I felt myself swing the steering wheel to a full left hand lock towards a steep downhill slope. But the car kept on going right ahead on the road. At that moment I heard a voice saying, "Straighten up son, I have a narrower path for you to follow. Go home!" And that I did, going home.'

'And over time your troubles lessened?' I suggested.

'Yes, I met up with the Man behind the Voice.'

'And your back got healed.'

'Yes, but that's a story for another time,' Dean said. 'I'll have to make tracks soon.'

'Sure.' That was fine by me. We would be meeting a few times yet before Dean's book was fully written.

'You know why I get disappointed when people love the miracles and not the invitation,' Dean said. 'I once understood so clearly that God loves us so much that he will do anything and everything to draw us to him. His intimacy, kindness and mercy towards us is so overpowering it is hard to imagine anybody could resist him.'

This reminded me of Lady Julian of Norwich (1342-1423) and her mystical visions which so clearly showed the incredible love of Jesus for everyone. Her favourite saying was that the Lord will do a great deed one day and make all things well for the whole of creation. The depth of God's love cannot be fathomed. But it can be readily ignored by people unless they are willing to engage with it.

'Human nature tends to be like that, it seems,' I said.

'Yes. Even Christians often seem unaware of how God can help them,' Dean responded.

'That's what you would like to tell everyone, isn't it.'

'I've decided never to give up on that. And thanks for your help, Michael. Perhaps that book we're working on may do some good.'

I had few doubts that indeed it might.

5

Healed!

When Dean arrived for our next chat he walked uncomfortably. 'Your arthritis from speed walking is playing up still,' I remarked. He confirmed it with a nod of the head. 'Those were crazy times, you know.' Dean sat down, made himself comfortable and began to tell his story.

'At 12 years of age I was at school looking out of my classroom onto the sports oval and saw this man continually walking very fast around it. That day, after school, I was training for the high jump. Once I had showered, waiting to be picked up by my father, the guy was still walking in large circles. I watch this happening for some weeks. In the end I simply had to interrupt him to ask what he was doing. That was the beginning of my walking.'

'You became quite successful.'

'Yes. I began riding my pushbike to various speed walking events and joined in. Over time I won some handicapped races and one Sunday morning my picture ended up on the front page of Adelaide's main Sunday paper. I was being presented with the winning trophy of a 40 km race by the president of the major South Australian brewery.'

'That was quite something.'

'It was. My dad happened to pick up that paper and suddenly I heard this almighty yell. It scared me witless; put the frights into me bigtime. He took off somewhere with me wondering what I would have done wrong. Back he comes with an old newspaper clipping and photo of himself. It turned out my father was himself a champion walker in his day and I never knew.'

'Surely, he would have known about you training for it?'

'He did, and my mother was always ready to cook me meals at the most ungodly hours, for training runs and races could end quite late. Dad was ever supportive, but never realised how good I was until he saw that paper. Perhaps he felt he shouldn't pressure me about the sport for it demands everything from you once you are committed.'

'Like being on a mission for God,' I suggested.

'Sure,' Dean agreed easily. 'There are quite a lot of similarities. From then on my father became my coach.'

'You were very fond of your father, obviously.'

Dean didn't answer right away and became quiet for a while. He must have been reminiscing over a man he lost far too early in life. I could identify with that, losing my dad at 16 years of age. You always wonder what might have been.

'He was a fine Christian,' Dean continued. 'I remember overhearing one of his prayer in his bedroom while I was standing at the door. I was only five years old. Dad was talking to Jesus saying "I don't mind what you do with me at all. All I ask is that you save my kids." Afterwards I was searching through his bedroom, even into the cupboard, trying to find this Jesus.'

'He is hard to detect at times,' I suggested with a smile.

'Yes. But while still at primary school I ended up at a crusade associated with Billy Graham. It was at the Wayville Showgrounds. All I know is that when the invitation came I ran up, hit the stage as one of the first to do so and tripping in the process. I kept on running and was about to fall off at the other end when a man caught me by the armpits. He said that I'd done well and would be used mightily in God's Kingdom.'

'How do you feel about that prophecy now?' I wondered.

Dean hummed a bit and didn't really like the question. 'I leave that for others to decide – the truth of it. I have few feelings about it. It kind of is what it is.'

'All I know,' he continued, 'is that I joined an external bible study program that made me work through the bible thoroughly. I was very committed to that.'

I drew the attention of the waiter and ordered us more coffee. The café had few customers that morning and soon a fresh brew arrived. In the meantime both Dean and I fell silent with our own thoughts. It was quite a story I was learning about. None of it had come up while I had been his Pastor. I had no idea how Dean found his Lord again once having lost the one of his childhood. I suggested to him that when he committed his life to Jesus as an adult, the Lord had not been actually foreign.

'That true,' Dean admitted. 'But I had little feeling for that. I knew of God, but not the living God, you could say. The One who makes a difference. My experience at Morialta Falls should have wizened me up to that, I suppose. But it didn't. I was too troubled. Nor was I familiar with healing prayer.

'Anyway, friends invited us to a Christian camp in Mildura and till this day I don't actually know why I went. It must have been a subliminal urge. I never really thought that it would be the start of my damaged back improving.'

'How about Kathy? What made her agree to join you?'

'She simply came along because our friends had asked.'

'So what was your back like?'

'Completely cactus. They were planning to do a risky operation as a final resort. Some people having agreed to such an operation found it not necessarily beneficial. Sometimes, it made matters worse. In 1980 medical skills were not supplemented by modern technology as today. I was booked in for the procedure to take place four days after the Christian camp.'

'But is was never done, was it?'

'No, it wasn't. And not because of any of my doing.'

'So, what happened?'

Dean stirred his coffee and took a sip.

'Kathy and I were booked into a caravan park with a community hall at its centre. We thought about using the time there for a holiday. Surely, we could do with one. But it worked out quite differently.'

Dean took another sip and shook his head to himself. I wondered what was to come.

'In the morning I walked to the showers with only a towel around my waist expecting soon to be back at our van all cleaned up. The path to the amenities lead past the hall with much glass along its sides and some doors that stood open to let the breeze through. I heard the speaker say: "Jesus asks for those who are burdened and heavily laden to come to Him and find rest." That rather simple sentence somehow changed everything – it changed my life. I had found the Man behind the Voice.'

'So you rushed to the shower to join the meeting afterwards?' I presumed.

'No.' Dean gave that hearty laugh. 'I stepped through one of the back doors towel and all and sat down. Didn't leave for a long time, transfixed by what I heard. Never made it to the showers. Kathy was annoyed once I got back to the van. We had planned to visit Mildura and she couldn't find me anywhere.'

That seemed like Dean. Impulsive, spontaneous and full on. It has served him well over the years.

'From then on we went to every meeting of that camp and there were quite a few.'

'Did you go to the front for healing prayers,' I asked.

'No, I didn't. When the camp days were nearing their end a total stranger approached inviting us for a barbecue at his house that evening. Going there completely changed my life from what it had been – spiritually, financially, physically and emotionally.'

That was a major a statement and just wonderful to hear.

'At one point, a young girl there said to me, "Mr Knight, the Lord told me you have some problems." I remember thinking, you don't know even half of it. Once contemplating suicide, possibly a vegetable in four days' time through an operation, making my wife's life a misery, you name it. A chair was pulled up in the middle of the people and I was asked to sit down.'

Laying hands on the sick and troubled is good New Testament practice. Obviously, it was what had happened to Dean.

'My mind tracked through all sorts of things during the prayers,' he explained. 'I had recently discovered that my father had been adopted. The cousins I had were not really true cousins. I was angry about not being told, but found myself forgiving him. Don't really know exactly what all went through my mind. Suddenly a great beam of light came down upon me and I couldn't get off the chair even if I had tried. I heard a strange noise also. It took a while to figure out that it came from my own mouth. I had been baptised in the Spirit and was loudly speaking in tongues.'

Glossolalia is a common spiritual experience in charismatic meetings and totally nothing strange to those who are able to utter such spiritual languages. I am one of them and would like to insist that it doesn't make me anyone special or particularly blessed. It is, however, a fine way of saying a prayer, with the Holy Spirit helping you to speak out important matters. Sometimes you sense what it is about. Often you don't, but accept it to be significant.

'Then we went home, Kathy and I,' Dean said. 'Something had changed drastically in my mind and body – that much I knew. I cancelled the operation as by the time I arrived home I was without pain for the first time since the war. I felt a strange kind of peace. It had a manner of aggression about it. Not like Vietnam where it was focused on people as the enemy, but now it seeks out the spiritual destroyer whom Jesus has dethroned once and for all on the cross. The Spoiler and agent of sin.'

Dean remained silent for a moment.

'That's the story of my healing,' he concluded and stared out of the café's window. A few customers came in through the door.

Some guy, this Dean.

More so, some Lord who guides him.

6

Paying the Price

Soon after his Holy Spirit baptism Dean went to be alone for a time of prayer and fasting. He told me it was not much of a hardship for him as his training for speed walking had involved all kinds of self-denying disciplines, such as getting up very early in the morning and hitting the road. These days he still gets up early every day not ever having needed much sleep. But now for prayer. One thing the Lord once revealed to him was that a dedication to God's purposes could be costly. Dean considered that a good test as to whether the Lord could trust him when directed to heal and perform miracles. Even Dean's worship demands much. He refers to King David, who in order to avert a plague, seeks to buy a threshing floor upon which to build an altar. It is offered him for free but David responded, 'I will not offer burned offerings to the Lord my God that cost me nothing.' (2 Samuel 24:24)

Countless times Dean must have appeared the fool for Christ. Suffering misunderstanding with people about his actions has occurred frequently. He himself would not always know what was to come having only partial insight into the Lord's guidance. In one situation this misunderstanding became painfully real in familial circumstances. A call came from Kathy's uncle one evening to say that his adopted son, Tim, had been arrested at the airport in Thailand in the possession of 5 kg of heroin. Could Dean pray?

'I asked the Lord my usual question, which has been given me at the start of my mission,' Dean said.

'This question is central to how you experience the Lord working with you?' I asked.

Dean nodded. 'Yes, it is. It is a prayer the Lord gave me for when I would be unsure about a given circumstance. The prayer is important to me. Perhaps you should write it in italics in my book.'

Father, in the light of what you know past, present and future, is their provision in your Word for Dean Knight

to do something here or should I step aside as you may have
somebody else assigned to do this?

'I learned to hear the voice of the Lord saying: Go, Stop, Wait, Later or whatever,' Dean explained. 'In the case of Kathy's cousin, Tim, I had a vision seeing the number six after which I saw him walking up his parent's driveway. Myself I saw running to the local chemist for a small throw-away camera and taking a photo of Tim to present him to a group of people.'

'They are very tough of drugs in Thailand,' I commented. 'He might have faced the death sentence.'

'He got life – all of one hundred years,' Dean answered. 'Anyway, I understood the vision and went to the family explaining that in six years' time their son would walk up the driveway for them to welcome him home. But he would arrive from Thailand in another Australian State first, not in Adelaide.'

'So what happened?'

'I began to pray Tim home. After some time his sentence was reduced. He became infected with HIV and ended up in hospital. The prison authorities must have thought his case to be one they could do without. Tim received the King's pardon and was sent home to die, arriving in Sydney not just with AIDS but also tuberculosis. In Sydney, because in those days it was the only place medically equipped to deal with AIDS. Tim's life was to end amongst the medicos.'

'How did the family take to that?'

'His father rang me saying scathingly, "So much for your vision of my son coming home." That hurt. I thought he could have been grateful for Tim at least being back in Australia.'

Dean had hung up angrily after that call and yelled at God about how the promise of Kathy's cousin coming home to Adelaide didn't seem likely to happen. Dean wondered whether he had failed somehow. God confirmed the homecoming gently, which calmed Dean down. Once more he began to declare the vision, given six years earlier, into reality. And sure enough, six weeks later Tim was released from hospital in Sydney, arrived in Adelaide and walked up his parents' driveway healed from tuberculosis and with AIDS apparently in remission.

'After Kathy's uncle phoned us about this home-coming, I ran to the shop for a camera to take some pictures of the event. Thereafter, I ended up on my knees before the Lord pleading for Tim's complete healing,' Dean explained. 'His health kept improving and not long after being back home he met a wonderful lady called Angel and was happily married. The Lord has a sense of humour.'

I thought of all this happening. Not that I could find the humorous side of it.

'For six years, I had the family telling me I was a horrid person giving their son false hope. It was a price I had to pay. Not just their scorn but hanging in there by faith, believing.' Dean was shaking his head.

I can only imagine what that took. For like us all, Dean is human with deep feelings and an ability to doubt. By all accounts he is an exceptional person.

'How do you manage to be spiritually that strong?' I wondered.

'Well, perhaps I'm kind of suited to it, I suppose. But more importantly, I have been specifically called by God. Don't ask me why. I never asked for it. And I have been trained by the Holy Spirit. It's like running a marathon that doesn't end. Not always pleasant.'

Dean reflected for a minute.

'I already mentioned that time of prayer and fasting soon after having been baptised in the Holy Spirit. It was the first of many fasts. That first time the Lord gave me my commission. At a beach shack, that was to become my frequent abode, I fell into a trance. An Apostle Paul like experience, I would think. The Lord told me that my life would be directed by his word, his voice, his presence and Spirit. That I would partake in heavenly directed experiences manifesting on earth. As with, "Thy will be done on earth as it is in heaven."'

And there was more.

'In this trance I was standing with a man on a precipice. All of a sudden he let a huge scroll unfold and it rolled right down the edge of the cliff. It had names on it. I asked him what it was all about. He answered that it was a record of all the people I would influence for God's Kingdom. Then I remembered something my earthly father once said. "When you go to be with the Lord in heaven, all you can leave behind on earth is your influence – make it good."'

'Your dad was a smart man,' I remarked.

'There is a bit more to the vision, which I'll tell you about some other time,'

Dean continued. 'The most amazing thing was, that just before coming back to earthly reality, I had a vision of the shack's front garden with an old fishpond, flowers and other things. I had arrived at the back through a brush fence – never been to the front. No guessing what I found once I opened the front door.'

The ways of the Lord are inscrutable and higher than our ways. His love and mercy are everlasting. The influences Dean has been spreading about would be of like quality. I sensed that he didn't like talking about himself and all that has happened while working for the Lord. He only did so because he felt thus instructed by the Holy Spirit.

7

Clarity and Fluency

Dean and I seem to drink a lot of coffee in this book, because we meet once a week mid-morning. He had just finished a fresh brew and was pouring me a cup with a fine aroma. As Dean sat down he began to tell me about a woman who one day walked into his office to buy life insurance. It eventuated that she was blind in one eye. The Lord had given him a scripture that morning which he prayed over her pressing his fingers into her forehead. Then he went to the kitchen to get them a cuppa (tea this time). All of a sudden he heard a shrill cry which caused the two cups to be dropped. Dean rushed back and this lady cried out, 'I can't see.' What have I done? Dean thought. The woman saw the terror in his eyes. 'No, I can't see with my glasses on and I can see with my left eye now also.' The Lord had given her perfect vision in both eyes.

Another time a female contact who sold Herbalife had been invited to speak at a convention of that company. She agreed initially but then realised she shouldn't have for she had a chronic stammer. In prayer that night, after Dean had heard of this disability, the Lord told him to phone this person in the morning and pray a scripture over her. She met with the organising committee to explain why her talk should be cancelled. At the end someone remarked that she had actually been speaking for almost 20 minutes without a sign of a stutter. The woman grabbed a book and began reading aloud very fluently. At the conference she was eloquent, spoke often, and included a report of her healing. She has never stammered since.

Dean told me the two verses from Scripture he had prayed as a healing blessing. Both from Isaiah 32 and written sequentially. 'Then the eyes of those who see will not be closed' (vs 3). Plus '…. and the tongue of the stammerers will speak readily and distinctly' (vs 4). Both these verses are part of a prophecy in Isaiah regarding the deliverance of God's people.

'It reminds me of the church,' Dean said. 'I often think that it sees with one eye and spectacles on and spiritually it stutters.' He seemed a little downhearted.

'After all these years in ministry you are disappointed,' I probed.

'Well, yes.' Dean mulled it over. 'My commission before God is to be primed by the Holy Spirit, get the Gospel out, and win the world for Jesus.'

'Surely, you have had success in that?' I said.

Dean didn't comment on that. 'When I told you about that vision of the man with the scroll there was a second part to it. It showed me that Christians must always be ready to rely on the Lord because inevitably in life, difficulties will arise. In these days, with the world a tinderbox of current and potential calamities, especially so.'

There was no denying that.

'God is willing to help and believers should tap into that. But many of them don't see it clearly nor are they eloquent in spirit. They're not equipped and often don't seem to be concerned about it either.'

Then Dean made a pertinent comment.

'We're in our mid-seventies, Michael. Have had

our run. I can't do much more. Perhaps that's why I want this book to be written.'

Dean had already once mentioned how he felt he had been enrolled into a different army from the one in Vietnam. This time into one that opposes spiritual principalities and powers. An image flashed across my mind.

'The book is to be your bugle call playing the Last Post,' I said.

Dean chuckled. 'Well, I trust it will blow for a long time.' He continued in explaining that, yes, he loved to tell people about the great things God can do. But more importantly, about what they can do for themselves if they will take God seriously 24/7.

'You mean, miracles are great but in a sense, so what?' I said. 'Of course, God is able to do such things, but the Lord would take more pleasure from people becoming relational with him.'

'Absolutely. Many folk have no idea what a difference that makes.'

'So, reading your book simply for its amazement value completely misses the point. Readers should seek to learn and walk with the Lord vibrantly.'

We had talked about that before. How much people liked it when Jesus fed them with loaves and fishes, but they shied away once he suggested they partake of his body and his blood. (John 6) A full stomach is nice, asking for an undivided commitment goes a step too far.

Dean nodded. 'So, what's the bottleneck, you think, Michael? Obviously, it's not a new problem and you would have considered it.'

I certainly had. How to see clearly according to God's nature and be eloquent in spirit. For that to be so, the Gospel must be well understood in its simplicity and magnitude, while the outworking of it in life needs a clear focus and continual effort over time.

'The bottleneck is human nature,' I said. 'Paul summed it up in Romans 7 with, "Oh wretched me!"'

'The dynamics of sin within us,' Dean remarked.

'Yes. Paul struggled against it and called on Jesus to help. The Apostle had a complete idea of what the Gospel was really about. Without him we wouldn't have a Good News. In his letters two matters shone brightly – Jesus as Lord and the believers being urged towards wholesome, decent living.'

'The Gospel is about Jesus, first,' Dean said.

'Right. But not enough of church life is focused primarily on Jesus as Lord, nor on the Holy Spirit as our Helper. That God's Spirit lives in us is a far greater miracle than all the healings God may do.'

'People don't realise the power that dwells within them,' Dean agreed.

'No, and often with their manner of life they will make a mockery of it. That's why Paul insisted on good living, again and again. Just read his letters.'

'I know.' Dean looked out into the garden at the back of his home. It was a gloomy, autumn day.

'I believe that good and caring living is a very spiritual thing to do,' I said. 'It is the foundation of all things truly Christian. A decent, principled life clears the spiritual eyes and purifies prayer. No dullness and stammering, but clarity and fluency.'

8

Pandemonium at Joslin

I knew that Dean had an incredible story to tell about Joslin and I asked him about it.

'That was years ago,' he said. 'But I should remember.'

Dean gave it some thought and I saw a smile on his face. 'It was quite crazy, you know. I wouldn't believe one word of it, had it not happened to me personally.'

That was quite an introduction.

'One day I was driving south to visit someone down the road when I heard the voice of the Lord say to me: "Turn around." I did and began travelling north in the opposite direction. I had no idea where I was going.'

'You just drove straight ahead?' I asked.

'No, not at all. I kept on turning corners heading

somewhere but not having a clue.'

'So where did you end up?'

'Northeast of Adelaide somewhere. I stopped at a large fence with a sign on it reading *Rehabilitation Centre*. I walked through the gate and down the driveway, absolutely being unaware of what was to come. It was sunny and after about 50 metres I saw people sitting around. It seemed peaceful enough.'

'But it didn't stay that way,' I figured.

'Heavens no! Suddenly I heard this loud cry shouting, "That's him; yes, he's here!" A guy comes running from a corner section of the building and throws his arms around me babbling as if possessed. I was totally at a loss as to what to do.'

Dean shook his head as if still in disbelief.

'When things settled down it turned out that the man's name was Robert. He told me he had just come back from the surgeon and was told he did not need an operation. "I'm going to live!" he said. I still didn't recognise him. Then he reminded me that I had prayed over him some time ago and it clicked with me what he was talking about. At some place well away from Joslin I had stopped to talk to him on impulse and I learned that he had an inoperable tumour. Now it was completely gone.

'He said, he had told people at the rehabilitation centre about it and then asked me how I knew he was there. I explained, that I had no idea but that the Holy Spirit had led me. Wow! He invited me to meet the people in the group he was living with. One was a Vietnam veteran like myself, another man had AIDS while a woman named Melissa suffered from a major breakdown.'

'It seems a place for mental as well as physical care,' I observed.

'Would have been. Anyway, as I open my Bible and begin to share my testimony with Robert three nurses carry Melissa outside on a chair and place her about three metres away from me. I had shared with Robert for about ten minutes when Melissa starts almost demanding that she wanted Jesus and kept on saying it. She gave the impression of being a little deranged and I tried to ignore her. Suddenly, it was like something thrust me towards Melissa. I asked her whether she would like to receive Jesus Christ as her Lord and Saviour. She grabbed me and said "please!"

So, I had her say a sinner's prayer after me. Then, all heaven broke loose and it was pandemonium. Tears flowing and people hugging each other. I asked Rob what was going on. He explained to me that everyone present had recited everything I said in that prayer, even the nurses. And so had he. I never had noticed and was over the moon. They all got saved and knew it. It took a while before I took my leave, I can tell you.'

I told Dean that, it being quite a happening, no wonder he had felt so elated. But he shook his head saying it was just the beginning of it.

'There was an unintended consequence, at least not suggested by me. The Lord seemed to have just warmed up,' Dean explained. 'I received a phone call that night telling me that the group I had prayed for was no longer willing to take their medication. They all said that they were healed. What best to do now? I suggested they assess how things are in the morning.

'Rob phoned me the next morning with an amazing story about Melissa. Apparently, she had been picked up from the street at the Adelaide Railway Station the day before. Her three children now were in government care with her father having kicked her out of his home long before. Then, Melissa comes on the phone. "Dean my father phoned me here explaining that he had just become a Christian and would like to pick me up. I told him about my own salvation. We spent time happy and crying on the phone."'

My Lord, I thought, but sensed the story wasn't yet finished. I was right.

'I went to see Melissa three months later,' Dean continued. 'Her children had been returned and she met a nice man. But there is another sort of miracle. How did her dad know where she was, having been only picked up the day before without fixed address? She had been away from home for some time. Now a Christian, her father wanted to search for his daughter. That day there was an unknown phone number on his desk. He had no idea where it came from. Deciding to call, he discovered that it was the rehab. I'm not sure whether the centre even knew Melissa's name at that point for she might have been uncommunicative. The father described his daughter and was told that indeed such a girl had just arrived.'

'How about the others?' I asked Dean.

'They all went home to their families that next day. Robert ended up joining a well-known evangelist traveling the world. The man with AIDS was healed. My ministry at Joslin continued for some time with good things following.'

Dean had begun this tale by saying that he would never have believed it but for being involved himself. It's not hard to see why.

9

The Dove

We were walking through the back garden into Dean's prayer den. It is a lined shed with a couch, some other seating, plus a table. It also houses a home gym with a bench and pullies and weights of all sizes. Exercise has remained important to Dean. 'Can't do that much anymore,' he grumbled. As if I hadn't found that out for myself some time ago. Dean spends a lot of time in this den starting early in the morning. He mentioned once more that sleep wasn't something he needed much of. Never had. Night was the time for serious prayer and reflection.

Not long ago something strange had happened when dawn was on the rise. It was a warm night and the door of the den was left ajar.

'I was wrestling in prayer,' Dean explained. 'It

lay heavy on my heart how much Christians do need the Lord. Of course, the world has always been full of strife one way or another. Many people don't have it easy. These days besides wars, famines and other calamities we are wrestling with COVID-19. That realisation hit me extra hard that morning and I was quite agitated in spirit.'

The way Dean described our world, he had every reason to be.

'All my life I have proclaimed Jesus, seen people born again and lives changed. Not close to what I would have hoped for, but that's the Lord's business. I have tried to be faithful. That morning though the spiritual poverty of the church in such uncertain times hit me hard. How little Christians are aware of the treasures in God that are available to them, whether they are in difficulties or not.'

'You hope your book will help,' I suggested.

'Yes, that's really what it's about,' Dean agreed.

We had discussed this before.

'Then while much agitated in prayer something happened which I'm still trying to understand and can become quite emotional about. Low and behold, while praying at early light, a dove appeared inside my den on top the gym. When I opened my eyes, I was flabbergasted. Where had that come from? My door was only slightly ajar. The dove just sat there looking at me, all peaceful and unconcerned.'

That was indeed unusual. Sometimes, my wife and I leave the glass sliding doors of our large balcony open. Then a bird that loses its bearings may fly in. It will become all of a flutter. Last week it happened with a pigeon while I was away from home that evening. My wife pointed out the down feathers on the floor everywhere. In the end the bird was tired out enough to be picked up and she released it outside. For a dove to fly in all calm and content, into a small unknown space, simply should not happen.

'I thought, Lord what's going on here,' Dean continued. 'In my spirit I felt kind of undone. It was too much. After a while I ran out of the door to get my phone from the house to take pictures. Once back, the dove was still there, all comfortable and at ease. Then it flew to the top of the ceiling fan. I sat down praying and it stayed for quite a while. Finally, the dove settled briefly near my arm as if to say goodbye and flew out of the door. I had a quick look and saw it go far away where it seemed to suddenly disappear.'

Dean had some photos on his phone and showed me a light brown/grey dove with some brown feathers, very composed and beautiful. I looked it up in a bird book later and could not find anything like it common to South Australia. 'What do you make of it,' I asked, 'that dove arriving?'

'I have thought about that a lot, of course. There is a message in that for me personally and I'm still praying that through. More generally though, the dove arrived after I had been agitating about the state of the world with God saying, "Tell them, they're going to need me." With the appearing of the dove things changed. My inner turmoil settled down into a strange but comforting and encouraging experience that still was kind of unnerving. The bird seemed so assured and so unruffled. Not in the least bothered or afraid. It must have been a representation of the Holy Spirit.'

'God telling you that all was under control.'

'Yes, but it was more than that. The dove seemed to convey that it would bring peace and control into anyone's life, if so asked.'

'You mean that God is willing and a very present help in trouble.'

'Yes. In my view you are a fool if you refuse to accept that invitation and reach out for it. But then, who am I?'

Then Dean made a comment that surprised me. 'That visitation of the dove is connected with the book we're busy writing.'

'How so?' I wondered.

'All this happened on Saturday early morning while I was in prayer also wrestling with how to make the book happen, for the Holy Spirit seemed to insist on it. Later that day I kept saying to myself "phone Michael!' Then Sunday morning, just before Kathy and I were leaving for church, you sent me a message on my phone about catching up. How about that? It really confirmed my feelings about the book.'

'Right.' It was all I said. I had not known this. Quite some time earlier, Dean and I had met for the first time after many decades and he mentioned the idea of writing a book then. Knowing the complexities of such an exercise and not aware of all that had happened to him since we had lost contact, I didn't much encourage him about writing. After that time we didn't stay in touch for Dean is always busy.

However, on the Saturday the dove was visiting, my wife and I sat on our balcony late afternoon in fine weather. I mentioned feeling uncomfortable with not having been more enthusiastic with Dean about a potential book. Perhaps I should have helped him. I sensed a prompting in my spirit about that while I had not given it any thought earlier. My wife agreed that perhaps I should have. So, I sent him a message about catching up. The Lord surely knows how to get things rolling again when necessary.

Throughout this conversation we had been standing in the den. Dean sat down on the couch before which on his knees he had spent uncountable hours in prayer. I took the straight-up chair to save my back. We just sat there for a while in quietness.

'Not many people are in contact with God like you are, Dean,' I said.

'It's all a matter of degree, Michael, and God doesn't do degrees,' Dean responded. 'Every sincere prayer is of equal value.'

'You mean, that someone doesn't need hours of prayer and fasting like you do to have God close.'

'No, of course not. That simply is my calling. Early in my walk God told me, "let us reason together" from Isaiah 1:18. I was invited to contemplate the ways of the Lord and my own disposition.'

'God is more interested in what you are really like, deep down, than in whatever you achieve,' I suggested.

'Absolutely. That's very much the key.' Dean became enthused. 'God is no respecter of persons but a discerner of the heart. Let us reason together. To do so honestly before God is the way to releasing the power of the Holy Spirit within you. Don't hide from God because of your own hang-ups. God knows who you really are anyway. Bring your hurts, insecurities and desires before the Lord openly and simply. There is no need for heavy prayers. I often just sit with God in mental discussion, run things past God and ask for help. Always in the knowledge that Jesus loves me and understands. There's no such thing as an angry God and surely not when you are transparent. God is love. I practise a relaxed humility. Spend little time on my problems which God is well aware of anyway. I simply wait before the Lord knowing that he will help, even though often it may not immediately seem so.'

That was quite a statement and the longest I ever heard from Dean. I had learned what he spoke about for myself and it is a good way to be. 'My ego is the destroyer of my peace,' I reflected.

'Yes. All those ego states must be avoided. God isn't into self-importance,' Dean agreed.

'So, what you just explained; that's how you build a sense of the Lord's presence 24/7 every day.' I knew that to be so in my own life.

'You do,' Dean said. 'That subtle sense of the Holy Spirit, who lives within you, being a Helper you can count on.'

We talked on a little more. About Dean's deep conviction that this is what Christians need to learn if they are to be properly equipped in a challenging world that could become 'unhinged'. I liked him using that word at times. God is willing and close. Will I be willing and feel personally close to God? As God told Isaiah: 'Let us reason together.'

10

Fact or Fiction

We were at a winery in McLaren Vale, an area south of Adelaide famous for its vineyards. Seated on a hill Dean and I could see for miles over rolling fields with the sea on the horizon to the west not far away. Our conversations about Dean's book had been mostly completed and the idea was to meet up for a relaxed lunch. The waiter had recollected the menus and food was on its way. A nice and calm autumn day made for a perfect outing on the winery's terrace.

Dean, ever the evangelist, posed a question. "Tell me the Gospel, Michael. The way you understand it.'

We had touched on it briefly before in our talks: how a proper understanding of the Good News helps you in being a Christian. Not always is it fully explained. Over the years I have given the Gospel some in-depth thought. Right now, it would be best to keep it simple because of time constraints. Basically, the Good News is simple anyway.

'It's a divine love story gone wrong with a happy ending,' I said.

Dean nodded and took a sip of mineral water. He was never a drinker of alcohol.

'God *is* Love,' I began. 'And the whole universe holds together in Jesus Christ as the first verses of John 1 and also Colossians 1:15 make clear. God's creative acts are not just lovingly done but rather our universe essentially is a manifestation of a God who *is* Love. It exists *in* Love.'

'God is the centre of everything,' Dean said after a moment. 'I get that.'

'For reasons we are never to know, when God created this handiwork it became fully infiltrated by a destructive power called sin. It brought suffering and death into the world – to all of nature. The influences of sin are far greater than merely moral failure. Love and sin are the two primary dynamics by which all of creation exists.'

'God would have known that, of course,' Dean suggested. 'That sin would infiltrate.'

'God created anyway. It must have been because

of a wonderful final outcome that otherwise could not be achieved. We cannot really know.'

'You mean our heavenly future.' Again, Dean nodded his head.

'Yes, but how to get there? Somehow sin needed to be done fully away with. Only the most powerful of forces could ever achieve it. It required not a word of command by God, but something far deeper: *an act of divine Love*. Only one Person qualified for such an act – the Son of God in whom, by God's command, all of creation came to exist.'

'That makes sense,' Dean said. He was enjoying himself. 'It exists in Christ and Christ saves it.'

'Love could not challenge sin arbitrarily. Love had to put its very nature in the balance and show the superiority of its essence. Love itself has no substance and neither has sin. So, a battle-like confrontation, how could that ever happen? It became possible by love becoming personified in creation. Also, it needed a battle ground at which love and sin exist as an intrinsic awareness that involves choice. The only place that qualifies for this is the human person in whom good and evil naturally coexist. Personhood became the place of facing off.'

Dean smiled. 'You almost sound like Star Wars.'

'Well, perhaps Star Wars has partly borrowed from the Gospel,' I suggested. 'To make this battle possible the Son of God became human. We know the Christmas story well enough.'

I paused for a moment thinking how to proceed.

'The battle against sin raged throughout Jesus' life and culminated at the crucifixion. Jesus needed to remain morally perfect and make all his choices in accordance with the nature of God.'

'Which he did,' Dean said.

'When on the cross, the personification of Love, Jesus Christ, faced off with that of sin in the form of Satan, the personification of evil. Satan belongs to the created realm. God the Father stayed out of the fight. As creation exists in the Son, it was Christ who would have to liberate it from the power of sin. On the cross the perfect love of Jesus Christ conquered and defeated sin once and for all. Jesus absorbed its power into his own person and nullified it in perfect love.'

My mind briefly reflected on how we will never understand the suffering that involved. It was of a divine magnitude. On the cross Jesus redeemed the whole of creation, every living creature, plant and tree.

'With sin being defeated, death also had been defeated,' Dean said. 'It had been defeated forever.'

'Yes. That was shown in the resurrection at Easter. From then on anything God created would no longer need to be marred by sin. A renewed creation became possible – one that would dwell solely in Love forever.'

Our meals arrived and we took time to enjoy it. The creation story was left alone for a while. The food was great and the small talk pleasant. After ordering a coffee Dean and I talked Gospel some more. I began.

'After the resurrection of Jesus something extremely significant happened. A pure spirit entered creation, being completely of love and none of sin. At one point all creation will come to exist in this spirit.'

'That existence is called heaven,' Dean said.

'Yes. Right now it is people first, who are invited into the dynamics of the pure spirit. Jesus explained it as being born again. Every person who takes this step

God declares worthy of the spirit's purity even though they remain living under the influences of sin while still on earth. A new dimension has been added into their very being. The personification of that pure spirit is the Holy Spirit.'

It is quite wonderful, really, I reflected. Of all religions, it is Christianity that recognises and deals with the power of sin once and for ever.

'Those who accept the invitation of Christ are expected to make the most of this privilege – this new life,' Dean said.

'Yes, they must develop the fruits of that new spirit, of the Holy Spirit. They have a special place in God's plan. Love has won and has claimed back all of creation. The true Christian is the beginning of that.'

Nothing worthwhile in life is ever easy. It requires dedication and persistence with always challenges and ideas that question things. The modern world is full of questions and answers, many of them dubious.

'You know what has helped me much in my Christian life?' I continued. 'Two things. Firstly, to know the Good News and its power. And secondly, how to remain convinced of that. Not making more headaches for myself than I need to.'

'What do you mean?'

'Well, I have learned a simple thing – that of accepting facts that I consider to be true, and Gospel facts are just that. Otherwise, why be a Christian? I never worry when it is suggested, even sometimes in my own head, that the Good News may actually be a clever fiction. To me, that God *is* Love is a fact. That Jesus is the Son of God is a fact. That he rose again, is a fact. That God's new spirit lives in me, also is a fact. As is the fact that I may tap into that. To me it is not a matter of whether I believe in all this. Believing has that fluid quality of shall I or shan't I. I live my faith by divine facts. I accept the fact and then believe in it. Not stupidly so, and only in matters that concern the Gospel, where doubting those facts will undermine the fabulous spiritual wealth God has given me.'

I enjoyed that, Michael,' Dean said. He looked contented.

Dean had arrived that morning from an appointment and we drove home in separate cars. That nudge of the

Holy Spirit upon me to lend Dean a hand with his book had rekindled a friendship. I would be faithful to the information given me while using a little poetic license where appropriate. I expected *I Am Willing* to become a good read. Quite amazing, really. About a God, who is ever present and closer than breathing.

More to Tell

As Dean Remembers It

My Favourite Poem

My life, my love I give to you,
You lamb of God who died for me,
Oh may I ever faithful be,
My Saviour and my God.

I now believe you do receive,
For you have died that I may live,
And now henceforth I trust in you,
My Saviour and my God.

Oh you who died on Calvary,
To save my soul and make me free,
I'll consecrate my life to thee,
My Saviour and my God.

I'll live for him who died for me,
How happy then my life shall be,
I'll live for him who died for me,
My Saviour and my God.

Ralph E. Hudson (1843-1901)

Back Problems

Standing in the kitchen one day I heard a voice telling me to phone a friend, whose wife soon would have back surgery to relieve the pain on her spine, even though the doctors were far from confident in solving the problem. For some time my friend and his wife had been fervently praying for healing. I asked him to do three things. Firstly, to go into separate rooms with their Bibles and note down three scriptures on healing. They should compare notes and the scriptures had to be exactly the same. If they were not they'd best forget about my call. Secondly, please take the X-rays and draw a straight line on it from the top to bottom of the back. And thirdly, within an hour forgive someone who has slighted you.

This they did. The scriptures were the same, they forgave someone who had offended them and my friend's wife felt a change in her body. This was on a Saturday. On Sunday at church I suggested they ask the Pastor for prayer. I was told it not to be necessary for the back had been healed. The operation was cancelled and years later the surgeon still couldn't believe what had happened.

A Tumour

Around that time I was speaking from the pulpit at my church and asked an elderly woman what she would wish from the Lord when told that God will do anything for her. She answered for the lady sitting next to her to be healed of a tumour. The seat that person occupied I had prayed over before the meeting as directed by the Holy Spirit. I prayed Matthew 15:13 over her. 'Every plant which my Heavenly Father has not planted will be uprooted.' The next Sunday the lady testified that the tumour was no more. Praise God!

Almost Deaf

In those days, I once called on a motor mechanic to sell him life insurance. He had been in a car accident in which a woman was killed. He himself came out of it with one completely deaf ear and the hearing in his other progressively deteriorating. Two surgeons were to arrive from Europe seeking a solution. I filled in the forms for him to sign and approached the insurance company for a life cover but they said no. Walking up his driveway to tell the bad news I heard a voice say,

'Lay hands on him and deliver him from this adversity.' I placed my hands on his head and said, 'In the name of Jesus Christ, I take away your hearing.' That was a crazy prayer over someone who had only partial hearing. As if I wished him totally deaf. I turned around and literally ran out of his driveway into my car. Soon I pulled over for I couldn't drive safely my legs were shaking that much. That evening Kathy took a phone call from a man who excitedly said to have been healed and now was able to hear the birds with both ears. At the surgeons office it was noted that both ear drums were functioning normally. They were not well pleased seemingly having come to Australia from Europe with no interesting operation to perform. And what about my silly prayer? I got the wording wrong and the Lord understood anyway.

Troubles unto Death

Walking the streets of Edwardstown, I was led by the Holy Spirit into a barber for a haircut. Once in the chair I heard the Lord whisper John 12:26 to me. 'If anyone serves me let him follow (pursue) me and where I am my servant will be also. If anyone serve me, him my

Father will honour.' The Lord impressed on my spirit that 'today I am here.' I took courage from that and asked the man if he had received Jesus as his Lord and Saviour. I didn't wait for his response but told him that God would deliver him out of his dilemma. I had no idea what problem I was talking about and left the salon convinced to have blown it. I continued working at insurance late into the night that day. Upon coming home Kathy had a mighty story to tell. The barber had phoned and told her that while sitting in his car with the exhaust being piped into the cabin in an attempt to commit suicide he heard a voice say, 'You have received Jesus as your Lord and Saviour!' It shot him out of his almost unconscious state. He jumped out, found my business card and phoned Kathy. She advised him to go to bed with the assurance that I would come over tomorrow. I then found out what this was all about.

Arriving at his home the car was still running and overheating with fumes everywhere. That took some time to fix. I learned that Kim was gay and had been dropped by his boyfriend. He just couldn't take it anymore. He had been brought up by his Christian mother and accepted the Lord in those days. His homosexual tendencies began to assert themselves much to his mum's disappointment. All this together made him decide to end his life. I ministered to him for a while.

Unfortunately, later Kim became involved with another boyfriend and became infected with HIV. He became very ill. One day Kathy told me just to bring him home to us. We'll take care of him. In this sickness unto death the Lord instructed me to speak Jeremiah 15:21 over Kim. 'I will deliver him from the hands of the wicked, and I will redeem him from the grip of the terrible.' As a result he was healed of AIDS and his life picked up from there.

Hands and a Tree

Again I walked the streets in Edwardstown and was led into a shop fitting company by the Holy Spirit. A woman asked me how she could help to which I replied that I had come to help her. She never flinched at that statement and just told me she had severe arthritis in her hands. They looked twisted and painful. I asked her to put her hands into mine. After she did I said,' You have placed your hands into the hands of Jesus Christ and he is going to heal you of your disability.' At that moment her husband stepped out of his office wondering what was going on. His wife suggested he go back to his desk explaining that I was healing her hands. He obliged and suddenly Lyn began to squeal, 'my hands, my hands.' Before our eyes fingers were straightening up and the puffiness of her hands normalised. She was aware to have had an encounter with the Lord. I asked whether I could pick her up the next day to go to church. She said, she'd love me to. When Kathy and I pulled up before her home the next morning a large gum tree lay in their front yard all cut up into pieces. What had happened?

When leaving her shop after the healing I commented that they should not be too surprised if something was to stop them from coming to church. Satan might seek to prevent it. That night in bed Lyn wondered what would happen if that massive tree fell on her house. Her husband Dave said it would go through them like a knife through butter. With that they heard a horrific crack and a bang. They raced outside and saw the large tree severed at its base. It had spread over most of their roof. Neighbours ran out and ended up helping to cut the dangerous branches into pieces. To everyone's amazement only a few tiles of the roof were cracked. We went to a local church in their district and halfway through the service Lyn cried out, 'Please, I must have Jesus in my life, now!'

Brain Tumour

Dropping into an accountant's office to say hello to John, an acquaintance, I met a man called Leon who had his business in the same building. He published glossy hardware magazines but was packing up to close up shop once and for all. I didn't even say hello but blurted out, 'Leon, do you want to receive Jesus Christ into your life as your personal saviour?' He answered, "Yes, I do." We sat down on a bench and I led Leon to the Lord, with him very sincerely saying a sinner's prayer after me. I learned later that he had no religious background at all. He had been shocked at his own response, but had felt that somehow he was receiving a second chance in life. The next day he phoned me at my office explaining that he didn't have his migraine last night. I said casually that the Lord would much use him in the Kingdom in the years to come. Leon then asked whether John had told me about his inoperable brain tumour. He had not long to live. Also his wife had left him two years ago taking their four years old son with her. I knew nothing about this. We hung up.

We had met on a Thursday and the following Monday afternoon Leon phoned me greatly excited about an unexpected call he had on Saturday from his wife. She suggested they meet up together. On Sunday after two years of separation they walked together as a family along the Torrens River discussing a new beginning. Six weeks later Leon was given a clean bill of health. He began to take his son to local soccer and after a year the family left for Croatia where a revival broke out.

Three Daughters

A friend of mine had asked me to visit Rick in a hostel in Adelaide. Rick was dying of cancer and I found him in a little room with simply a bed, a small table and a chair. I walked in without saying hello and asked what he would ask for if Jesus turned up. I had Mark 10:51

impressed into my spirit where Jesus asks the blind man what he would want him to do for him. 'I want to see my three daughters before I die,' Rick said. But more so he wanted to see Jesus. We shared the sinner's prayer where after I thanked the Lord for Rick's three daughters to contact him. I learned later that at that very hour his daughters wondered where their father was, whether he even was alive. They began phoning each other, two living in Sydney and one in Brisbane near their mother. They rang many authorities until they found Rick in Adelaide. They had not seen their father for four years. Within three days one daughter came visiting him. After discussing it with the rest of the family it was decided to bring Rick to Brisbane. On the big day all three sisters arrived to collect their father. That morning Rick climbed out of his bed and walked down the stairs, which he had not been able to do physically for three months, in a new suit he had bought. That morning, my friend and I watched on as he boarded the plane to Brisbane where his wife lived with another partner but had a house available for Rick to live in. He began going to church to worship and after 12 years the Lord took him home.

A Morning Run

A friend of mine asked me to come to Strathalbyn to pray for a man called Peter who had AIDS. He looked weak and gaunt. I asked him whether he considered himself to be a sinner in need of salvation. He said, 'Yes, can I be saved?' My friend had ministered to him a few times previously. We recited the sinner's prayer asking Jesus into his life and heart. I told him God had healed him and left for home. Waking up the next morning all pain had left his body. Upon asking to go home he was told he was too sick for that – he had not been out of bed for some time. He decided to go home anyway.

When nobody was around Peter climbed out of his bed and walked out of the hospital. Someone had seen him moving fast across the carpark. Peter was making his way home to Meadows, 18 km away. The hospital sent out an ambulance to fetch him. At one point he hid behind a tree and without success the ambulance turned back. Once home in Meadows Peter asked his male friend to leave.

Over time, Peter set out to become an Anglican priest. He became baptised in the Holy Spirit. For quite a while I took him to the Full Gospel Business Men's meetings. Peter in a nice suit with his cross on the lapel looked quite the ambassador of Christ.

Peace

Kathy and I were visiting Ingrid and her husband when a call came through from Darwin. It was Amelia, a business contact whom Ingrid had ministered to in the past. Amelia was most upset as they had sold their house to move to Brisbane for her husband Victor's new job. With the removalist truck all packed to go the news arrived that this job had been cancelled.

Ingrid had no idea how to respond to this bad situation but told Amelia that a friend was visiting who could help with prayer. I was reaching out to God for inspiration with this desperate lady on the line. I felt to lead her to Christ and guided her through the sinner's prayer, after which I told her that the problems they were facing were now not hers but the Lord's. Ingrid was quietly praying herself all that time and the Lord showed me it was her faith that though small like a mustard seed had moved his heart.

Within the hour Amelia called back. Competitors

of the company Victor was going to work for were offering him a job instead with all relocation costs paid for and much better wages. Where they got Victor's contact details is unknown to this day. He would work on an oil rig.

This is not the end of what God did for Amelia and Victor. I kept them in my prayers unawares of what was to follow. A good time later I received a letter with Amelia explaining how increasingly Victor had become impossible to live with due to stress. On Friday 25 January 2002 he came home for a ten days break after having been at work for 28. Amelia had decided that it was the time she would raise the possibility of them separating. Victor became exceptionally violent at this suggestion and with the children looking on in horror vandalised their house. 'He tried to choke me to death; only stopped when our 14 years old son pulled him off,' Amelia wrote. Then Victor swallowed over 100 blood pressure tablets and became unconscious. Arriving at the Tweed Heads hospital he was found dead once on the treatment table with the medical staff busy trying to revive him.

During this time of unresponsiveness something

amazing happened, Amelia explained in her letter. God showed Victor his life to date, the good and the bad, and what actually it could be like depending on his choices. 'God spoke many things to him in this time,' she wrote, 'all of which have been confirmed by you and people in our church absolutely word for word.' Victor regained consciousness and late that night called Amelia at home telling her in exact detail what had happened to him while being unconscious. What God had shown.

Victor accepted Christ, was baptised a week later, and found himself changed completely much to Amelia's amazement. She and her children had never known such peace. 'Victor knows God now in a way most only dream of,' Amelia conveyed. 'A miracle happened and we were in it – how awesome!!!! God is awesome. He has a reason for everything and sometimes takes a person to the point of death to achieve His plan. … I have learned that God has NO limits, only we limit Him.' The opening sentence of Amelia's letter reads: 'Here is our testimony, I hope it helps someone!!! It really helped us!!'

Interlude

Dear Reader, please stop for a minute and take stock. Ask yourself what your Christian life is really like and what it could be potentially. Does the communication between you and your Lord flow freely? Are regular prayers with openness and humility happening? How long since you have read from the Bible? Or have sat with God quietly in reflection? Do you have the Lord in the background of your thinking often during the day? And what is your attitude like towards people and towards your own health? So many challenging questions. And why bother? Well, simply because a relationship with Jesus, that is truly a relationship, makes life more bearable. Better still, it makes it worth living. Just think about it.

Unbelievable

A friend of mine, called Wayne, had diabetes and also a hole in his heart that finally was to be operated on. During this difficult procedure his heart stopped with the surgeons, after much trying, unable to resuscitate him. Wayne was declared deceased and was about to be wheeled away. This was in the afternoon.

I was not aware of his operation happening. While working in the garden together with Kathy in the morning of that day the Holy Spirit told me to go to my den, get on my knees and pray a certain scripture over Wayne. Three times during that day I was thus prompted by the Lord. It occurred to me that what I expressed in prayer were things Jesus would say when raising the dead. I prayed to the point of finally saying, 'enough - this far and no further. Wayne, wake up.' I felt my task to be finished still having no idea what it was all about. That night a mutual friend phoned and said, 'Dean that was an amazing thing you did for Wayne.' I asked what had happened and he told me the story.

The following day I was painting the back room with Sean, my son, and Wayne arrives. In his usual jovial manner he throws his arms around Sean and myself with Kathy also present. Wayne asked me how I managed to get into the hospital to minister to him as nobody would normally be allowed into the operation theatre. 'And you were wearing pretty much what you've got on now,' he said. Kathy told him that I had not been to the hospital but had been in the garden and the prayer den. Wayne couldn't believe it. 'This is what you said when you stood over me,' he said, and he repeated word for word my main prayer for him right up to when I had told him, 'You are free, wake up.' And that is what he did on that hospital bed having been considered well and truly dead and ready to be wheeled away. The staff did not believe a word of Wayne's testimony and said it would not be recorded in his case file. Another surprise was that Wayne was healed of his diabetes though the hole in his heart was never fully fixed.

The Scarf

One evening I was unusually tired having my dinner when Kathy took a call. She told me that I was needed urgently on the phone. I suggested she take a message instead, to which Kathy responded that I must take the call. I found myself connected to a woman in Sydney and another in an ambulance simultaneously. I could hear the sirens blaring. The person from Sydney had been ministering to a friend whose child was now being rushed to hospital and had told the friend that if she phoned me all would be okay. I could hear a man in the ambulance say to the mother that unfortunately they had lost the young child. 'I'm sorry Mr Knight,' she said almost casually, 'you can't help me now.' In my spirit I responded that indeed she was right in that I couldn't help her, but Jesus could. I asked whether she had a scarf, which she did. Put it over your son's face and gently blow over it, I instructed her. As she did so, I commanded his breath to return which it did. Upon arrival at the hospital the ambulance people were accused of negligence for their respirator was not attached to the child. They explained that it was not necessary as a man of God had prayed over the phone and the child had come back to life. The surgeons found nothing wrong with the boy and allowed him to go back home completely healed.

Josiah

In a similar situation Kathy received a phone call late at night from a friend in Alice Springs explaining that their daughter was flying from Darwin to Adelaide with their baby of a few weeks in an emergency they didn't have the necessary equipment for up North. I had once ministered to the whole family without them being responsive. Now I was asked to pray for the baby boy, who as yet didn't even have a name. Kathy urged me to pray and I said no. She upbraided me that they were her friends and I must pray. I succumbed, climbed out of bed grumbling, and knelt down in the living room using a prayer the Lord had given me on previous occasions. 'Lord, in the light of everything you know, is there provision in your word for me Dean Knight to have anything to do with this situation.' All of a sudden from the depth of my stomach and on the top of my voice I yelled out, 'Josiah!' I ran back into the bedroom and asked Kathy for us to pray together for God was going to do something supernatural.

We worked out later that the doctors and nurses were trying to resuscitate this now unresponsive child and at the moment I yelled out his name the baby woke up feeling well. It was also then that the mother felt the boy's name impressed upon her by the Holy Spirit. He would be called Josiah. We later received a fine card expressing his parents' gratitude.

Steady Ahead

While preaching at a church in Sydney the Holy Spirit

had me look over at a couple and told me to step down from the pulpit, prophesy over the man, and heal him. I had no idea who he was. The Lord had me tell him that he was to heal people, especially young ones with major bodily disabilities, heal their souls. The Lord would give him increased faith to do greater things than he was already doing in honour of God. The congregation seemed awestruck. I was surprised and inquired with the Lord what to do next. I asked the man to stand up and walk around the building. This he did and it stirred even more excitement. People were standing on their feet praising the Lord and clapping. I was still none the wiser what was going on until the Pastor came up to me almost laughing and explained what was happening. It turned out that the man was a top gynaecologist in Sydney but all this life had felt to broaden his skills as he himself had suffered polio as a child. He always had a limp because one leg was shorter than the other. But now he was walking around without any of that, his legs being of equal length. I remained in Sydney for a week, which this doctor took off work to support my ministry. It became one of the weeks in which I experienced God doing many things. One of my best in serving the Lord.

Simply Gone

I was asked to preach in Middleton, a seaside town south of Adelaide. I had been there once before and prophesised over a woman who couldn't conceive and since that day had become the mother of three healthy children. Anyway, I felt the Holy Spirit lead me to fast often over a period of 90 days from the day of the Middleton invite. The service had only just begun when I was allowed to share. I told the congregation about my fast and the belief that God was going to do something special today. Immediately the church elder's phone rang and he became apologetic – I said don't be for God is at the other end. He took the call near the microphone so it became amplified. Excited voices shouted through what had happened. Some of the elder's family members in Sydney had visited a Red Rooster restaurant when they noticed a family with a very young daughter who had a large tumour on her head. Their own daughter, who was only 11 years old, casually walked over, put her hands on the tumour and spoke it away in Jesus' Name. In view of everyone at the restaurant the tumour shrunk and disappeared. I remember saying, 'well, how do you beat that?' The morning service continued till 3 pm that day.

Wicked and Wonderful

After one of my regular periods of fasting I was asked to meet the day after tomorrow with some men to pray for a 14 years old boy who had leukaemia. From the moment of the invitation I was carrying the boy's health in my spirit. When watering the garden the power of the Lord came upon me from Ezekiel 16:6-7. 'When I passed by you and saw you struggling in your blood, I said to you in your blood: Live! I made you like a plant in the field and you grew matured and became very beautiful and fruitful.' These verses I ended up prophesying over the boy while in prayer with those men. That night his blood count was back to normal. He had been healed of leukaemia.

There is more. A year later I was contacted by a man and asked to come to his home at the other side of town. When I asked why, he simply urged me to come. It got my curiosity going. When I turned up at this stranger's home, he sat me down in a large chair. There I waited sensing that I would meet some people. After a while five of the most beautiful women I have ever encountered at one sitting were ushered in. It made me feel rather uncomfortable. What was happening here? They sat down, everyone facing me, and one of the women spoke. 'Mr Knight,' she began. 'We are witches and have just returned from a conference in India discussing something important to us. It's about Tim.'

I gulped and my mind went in overdrive. I knew of a few Tims, I had healed. Which Tim were they talking about? Not wishing to appear clueless I responded with 'Uhuh.' The woman let me off the hook. 'We have been praying for a year to our Master for Tim at Victor Harbor to be healed of leukaemia. We were assured our God could heal him. We knew the family and expected to show that our religion was the one to follow. But we couldn't heal him. Then you come along and in one hour Tim is healed from that disease.' I asked impulsively why the darkness of their Master would work against itself. That was pretty smart, I thought, and wondered where it came from. Another of the women queried what I meant. I understood that they hadn't invited me to challenge their faith and felt to be in trouble. I quickly prayed on how to respond.

One woman was sitting quietly to the side. I looked at her and began to address her as if there was no-one in the room. 'You are painting a mural but do not have the money to finish it. Please say how passionate you are about it.' She responded in telling me that she had a dream given by a God foreign to her. I told her that was Jesus, who was going to show her that he was the one and only God by supplying the means to finish her artwork. Please contact me when it is done and we will further discuss it, I requested. I then continued to tell the story of a king's servant who had found the one true God but was forced to worship the gods of the king. Asking of a prophet what to do for he felt uneasy about this, he was advised to just continue what he was doing. The one true God looks at the heart and not the rituals. That very God always protects the true worshipper with a powerful love. I felt to have gained the attention of the women as they never asked another question.

Two weeks later I received an incredible letter in the post including a cut-out from the local newspaper with the heading: Miracle Worker's Virtue Rewarded. The mural painter had received an envelope with $7000 placed under her door. Most encouraging was that the girls came together later on and accepted Jesus Christ as their Lord and Saviour.

Please take note, Dear Reader
Sensationalism is not a biblical word,
Nor does it reflect the nature of God,
Let us avoid it.
Not all has been told by me, but it should suffice,
For us together to exclaim,
HOW GREAT THOU ART!

Wishing you well, in Jesus our Lord,

Dean Knight

I Am Willing is about an evangelist; a man of God with the gift of healing doing miracles, who pays a heavy price for his divine commission. In his ministry Dean never suggests the person prayed for needs to have sufficient faith for great things to happen. The faith is with Dean, when he senses a movement of the Holy Spirit. As Jesus said, 'I'm working because I see my Father working still.'

It would be nice to have someone like Dean living next door, but that misses the point. Dean is called to help one and not another, which is not of his choosing and is the Lord's business. Dean himself suffers from a painful hip and a vulnerable back these days. Physician heal thyself?

I Am Willing hopes to show that life can be lived with God close-by without there being a Dean around. A God who may do a miracle, but more so, when asked to become involved, is a Helper in everything that life may dish up. There are many minor 'miracles' in a Christian's life that easily go unnoticed, when God guides and provides.

Therefore, be strong and confident. The God who helped Dean greatly will help you likewise in your struggles. It has been a pleasure to make this book happen.

Michael J Spyker
Adelaide, 2021